W9-ADC-582

YOU
Can Talk
to
(Almost) Anyone
about
(Almost) Anything

CEDAR CREST COLLEGE LIBRARY
ALLENTOWN, PA. 18104

YOU
Can Talk
to
(Almost) Anyone
about
(Almost) Anything

A SPEAKING GUIDE FOR
BUSINESS AND PROFESSIONAL PEOPLE

---

by
Elaine Cogan
and
Ben Padrow

Continuing Education Publications
Portland State University
Portland, Oregon

© 1984 by PADCO. All rights reserved.

This book, or any part thereof, may not be reproduced by any means written or mechanical, or be programmed into any electronic retrieval or information storage system without written permission from the publisher, except in cases where short passages are used solely for the purpose of review in periodicals, television, and radio.

First Printing October 1984.

Library of Congress Cataloging in Publication Data

Cogan, Elaine, 1932-
    You can talk to (almost) anyone about (almost) anything.

    1. Public speaking. I. Padrow, Ben, 1927-
II. Title.
PN4121.C557   1984   808.5'1   84-15531
ISBN 0-87678-021-4
ISBN 0-87678-022-2 (pbk.)

Segments of this work were published in *Oregon Business Magazine*.

Designed by Susan Applegate, Publishers Book Works, Inc., Portland, Oregon
Illustrated by Kathleen Deal.
Author photograph by Dan Poush.

Manufactured in the U.S.A.

Published and distributed by:
Continuing Education Publications
Portland State University
1633 S.W. Park Avenue
P.O. Box 1491
Portland, OR 97207

To
Aristotle and Cicero
In Whom We Believe

and

Glen and Our Dear Families
Who Believe in Us

FOREWORD
by
United States Senator Bob Packwood
State of Oregon

Occasionally, and only occasionally, there comes forth a book so clear, so cogent—and usually so short—that it is a gem. *You Can Talk to (Almost) Anyone—about (Almost) Anything: A Speaking Guide for Business and Professional People* is one of those books.

In relatively few pages, Elaine Cogan and Ben Padrow have captured the essence of what can make you a good public speaker. You'll be able to marshal your facts with intelligent foresight. You'll be able to deliver your message with conviction and effectiveness. You won't necessarily be a great public speaker. That's the upper one percent of public speakers. That's the William Jennings Bryans and the Franklin Delano Roosevelts. You achieve that if you not only follow the principles of this book but have a certain IT that cannot be learned from any book. Without hesitancy, however, I can guarantee that if you follow the principles of this book, you will never make a terrible speech.

Based upon a lifetime of public speaking, I can assure you that all of the things the authors catalog that can go wrong, will go wrong. Whether it be slides inserted in the projector tray upside down, or the master of ceremonies tripping over the microphone cord effectively disconnecting you from an audience of five hundred, or the introducer who says, "You all know Bob. Well, Bob, why don't you stand up and say a few words;" this will all happen ten times over. Ninety-nine percent of it can be avoided with preparation. This book will prepare you. What Julia Child is to cooking, this book is to public speaking. Read it, digest it, use it, and you'll be invited back to speak again. Fail to use it, and the audience will most likely wonder why you were ever invited the first time.

In addition to the principles enunciated in the book, I can speak from personal experience with one of its authors, Ben Padrow. When I first ran for the United States Senate in 1968, he gave me cogent and timely advice on both public speaking and appearances on television. In a race that was won by the slimmest of margins, any one of dozens who helped me tremendously could say they were the difference. In Ben Padrow's case, he was certainly a factor beyond compare because he took the time to teach me orally what he and Elaine Cogan have set down in writing.

* * *

CONTENTS

You Cannot Not Communicate

INTRODUCTION

"Jim, I agreed to give a speech about the breakthrough we made on the last case, but I've suddenly got to fly to Denver. Will you do it for me? There's nothing to it. Thanks."

Who can say "no" to the boss? It doesn't take too much persuasion to get you to agree to be his substitute. But now that you have said yes, you will make a speech in public, panic sets in.

Will you have something to say? Will the audience want to hear what you have to say? What will you do when your mind goes blank?

We hope it is some consolation that you are not the only one who feels nervous and uneasy when you have to give an oral presentation. In fact, in a recent survey, forty percent of the population says they are more afraid of giving a speech than getting cancer or a heart attack! Whether we have to make a presentation to clients, a report to shareholders, a pep talk to employees, an address to trade or professional associates, or a speech to the local Rotary, Kiwanis, or PTA—whether we are novices or experienced—most of us are apprehensive.

The first maxim you should remember is that subjects don't bore people. People bore people.

Unfortunately, too many individuals are highly educated in their field but do not take the time and effort to learn how to present that information well in an oral situation. They read twenty pages of single spaced text, or fumble through a jumble of hastily assembled notes. Their delivery is so poor or disjointed that the audience finds it nearly impossible to follow.

The second important point is that no audience wants a speaker to fail. However, it takes work to learn how to present our ideas clearly and deliver them with wit and style.

But, just as we did not become experts in our fields overnight, we cannot expect to be natural orators. We can learn, however, and that is what this book is all about.

Help is at your fingertips! To be a successful speaker, it is not necessary to enroll in a course in public speaking or read a five hundred page tome. Just follow the hints on the following pages and you will reap rewards you never dreamed of. You will get the satisfaction of seeing your audience smile, nod in agreement, and wonder where you got your training.

We won't tell. It's all right with us if you keep the secret to yourself and never admit you learned it all from this little book.

We are delighted to pass on the information we have learned as teachers and consultants in oral and written communications and which, until now, we have shared only with selected clients.

When Ben speaks, people listen . . . when he speaks out about public speaking, they pay attention.

He not only has been a professor of speech communication at Portland State University for thirty years, but also is a radio and television commentator and a consultant to corporate and political leaders in the highest levels of business, industry, and government. He is sought out by people who want to be winners and know that proper speech composition and delivery will give them that edge. Ben was cited recently by an Oregon Supreme Court Justice as one of the two greatest influences on her professional life. He coached a national award-winning General Electric College Bowl team, and has taught a generation of students how to command attention with the spoken word.

Elaine is a professional writer and consultant on communications to business and professional people. She is a radio commentator on public affairs and was producer/host of a highly rated talk show for nearly seven years. Elaine writes, produces, and moderates cable television programs, and is a weekly editorial columnist for *The Oregonian* newspaper.

This book is organized so it can be read straight through, or opened to just the one or two chapters which cover the subjects that may be giving you trouble. Thus, if you need help organizing, turn to Chapter 2, *Put It All Together—Organization Is All*. If you want to know how to use visual aids, then read Chapter 5, *Replace Your Thousand Words with a Picture*. In each case, you will find hints you can adapt with ease and confidence to your own style and situation.

Remember, *You Cannot Not Communicate*. Everything you do and say conveys a message about who you are and what you believe. Learn to communicate well, and you will be well on your way in your chosen business or profession.

Elaine Cogan and Ben Padrow

40% of the population says they are more afraid of giving a speech than getting cancer or a heart attack

JANIE DOE

SPEECHMAKER

DIED OF
FRIGHT

1

Rules of the Road

Subsequent chapters provide specific guidance on how to prepare and deliver a winning oral presentation. First, however, it is important to put yourself in a positive frame of mind.

*

Start out with self confidence. If you are being given the podium by virtue of your position, i.e. president or department manager, you did not rise that high without being someone special. If you have been asked to deliver a speech on a specific topic, someone believes you have had enough experience and training to impart useful information to a particular audience. If you are making an important presentation to potential or current clients, you have been chosen spokesperson because of some special expertise or knowledge. In other words, you have something to say to an audience which is waiting especially to hear from you.

*

Though some parts of your speech may be transferable to another occasion, unless you are a politician on the stump, never give a canned presentation. At the least, you risk having someone in the audience hear it twice. Always personalize your approach. If the group is generally unfamiliar to you, take time beforehand to find out as much about them as possible. Ask the person who asked you, or read an annual report. Try to find out anything which will help you know them better, and tailor your presentation to them. Their average age, sex, socioeconomic and educational levels, and reason for being there are especially helpful pieces of information.

*

Never give a canned presentation

Show what a truly human being you are by inserting personal anecdotes where appropriate. *(Why, just last week this happened to me . . . To illustrate my point let me tell you about myself . . . or By doing it this way, we found that . . . .)* If members of the audience can relate to you and your experiences, they will forgive—if not forget—those inevitable flubs and foibles.

*

Do everything you can to bridge the inevitable physical and psychological gap between the speaker as the guru/expert and the audience as the uninformed receiver. Use personal pronouns such as *we, us,* or *our.* Avoid any circumstances which give the impression that the audience is "you folks out there" and that you consider yourself more important.

*

Remember that the spoken word is naturally more informal than the written word. Therefore, contract and combine whenever possible. *We're* is better than *we are; can't* should be substituted for *cannot.* There are times, however, when you will want to separate words for emphasis. *We cannot do this* is much stronger than *we can't do this.*

*

Never forget that listeners have only one chance to understand what you are saying. They do not have a written page that they can re-read at their leisure. Help the audience keep track of what you are saying by numbering your points clearly—*one, two* or *first, second.* Add expressions to help them follow along such as *next, now, since, moreover, on the other hand,* or *Let's look at the subject another way.*

*

Speak in a conversational tone but not at a conversational speed. A good rule of thumb is that it should take you from ninety seconds to two minutes to read a double spaced, typewritten page.

*

Refresh yourself—and your audience—by carefully planned pauses.

*

Do not hesitate to give your opinion. *It appears to me . . . From my experience . . . I think that this is the correct way . . . .* For the brief half hour or so of your presentation, you are the expert. Act the part, but do not overact.

*

As expert as you are, however, many times your argument may have more weight if it is backed up by another authority who happens to agree with you. But choose the person or source carefully. It must be someone who is credible to your particular audience. In general, the president's opinion is more appropriate than that of Henry the Eighth, unless you are speaking to the Daughters of the British Empire or to members of the opposing political party.

*

Avoid obscure or esoteric references. It may boost your ego to show the listeners what you know that they do not know, but they will not like to be reminded. Even though they are unlikely to show open hostility, audiences have a way of getting back at a speaker who talks above their heads and lets them know it. They will stop listening, be unresponsive, or, horror of horrors—not buy your product nor hire you or your company.

*

Use metaphors, analogies, and anecdotes to lighten up your message—but only when they are appropriate to the subject and suited to your style. Avoid the trite and often inappropriate opening joke.

*

Remember that people are persuaded more by logic and reason than by emotion. That doesn't mean you should eliminate exaggeration and hyperbole entirely; just use them carefully. Words such as *magnificent, tragic, awful, greatest, worst,* are useful . . . but only when you are making a special point. Do not overdo it.

*

Cultivate a personal rhythm and delivery which is pleasing to the ear and characteristic of you.

*

Be assured that no audience wants a speaker to fail. After all, he or she is taking up one of their most important possessions: time. Most of them probably are grateful just because they are not in your shoes. Speaking terrifies them, too. Capitalize on their good will by appearing to be relaxed and confident. If you follow the steps in this book, you will be.

* * *

2

Put It All Together

ORGANIZATION IS ALL

By now, you should be convinced you are the right person to give this oral presentation, and you know enough about the audience that you can formulate a message which speaks directly to them. Notice, however, that you have not yet put anything on paper. Do not panic.

Ideally, it is now three weeks before your scheduled presentation. If you have less time, you will have to work faster. If you have more than three weeks, forget the speech until that time, or try to.

By the end of this chapter, if you have followed our rules, you will have written a complete twenty or thirty minute presentation which covers all the material you need to say at this particular time. Notice we insist that it be no longer than half an hour. That rule is based on long experience. The only instance we know of where length is rewarded and brevity is suspect is a meeting of academicians.

Never forget that the attention span of the average adult is two and one half minutes. Even though most audiences are polite and will not just walk out, they will begin to fidget, cough, roll their eyes, and otherwise show their inattentiveness after sitting still thirty minutes. Even if you are certain you have more information than can be conveyed in that amount of time, restrain yourself. You can distribute it as a handout that the audience can read at its leisure. Or, you may be so good that the group will ask you to come back and you can present everything you left out the first time!

Save some of this additional information for the question and answer period which you should consider a logical extension of your speech. A speaker who is not willing to answer questions is immediately suspect, as the audience wonders what he or she has to hide. Being willing to answer questions marks you as someone who has confidence enough to risk facing the unexpected. But you will be prepared—more on that later.

We suggest a rather unorthodox way of compiling your material, but it is a proven formula for success. Our method has many advantages. It releases you from the traditional system which stifles your creativity and allows you to take full advantage of your knowledge, skills, and precious time.

*

The first step is to meet with a representative of the sponsoring group to choose your general subject. This can be accomplished when the initial invitation is extended, usually in person or on the telephone. Within a general topic, try to have as much flexibility as possible to choose the specific information that is most likely to interest this particular audience, and also, that you know well.

*

When you begin to put thoughts to paper, resist the temptation to start writing your speech from beginning to end. First write down everything you know about the subject without bothering with the order or the form—just put it all down.

*

Always carry writing paper and a pencil or pen so you can jot down random gems as they come to you. Some really organized types put everything on notecards. Others scrawl on matchbook covers, paper napkins, placemats, or scraps of paper. It is not important what you use, but it is important to capture all your brilliant ideas. For later ease of organization, limit your thoughts or pieces of information to one per piece of paper.

*

Use your spare time to advantage by programming your brain to thinking about your speech. Put it on automatic pilot so that it clicks on when you are engaging in routine activities—riding to work, eating lunch, taking a shower, going on errands, or waiting for your child to finish a music lesson. Your thoughts are wandering anyway; think idly about the contents of your speech and you will be surprised about how many good ideas will come to you.

*

Jot down random gems

Be receptive to your surroundings. The best ideas come from seemingly unrelated sources—a billboard or bumper sticker, random conversation in the supermarket checkout line, a newspaper headline, television, radio, a book. Later on, you will incorporate these ideas into your speech so that they are uniquely your own, but now, just write them down. The more raw material you have, the better.

*

All this culling and mulling should take no more than a week. You may find that you know volumes about one subject but are skimpy on some other details. Do not waste your time going to the library and consulting the oracles. That research will come later, if at all.

*

It is now about two weeks before the date of your presentation—time to get serious. Plan to spend half the remaining time writing the speech, and the other half perfecting its oral quality.

*

Now, assemble all those thoughts and ideas. Spread them out on a table or the floor. This should be easy if each has been written on a separate paper. If not, you will have to take the time to rewrite them.

*

Look them over. Move them around as you would a deck of cards until they are assembled in a logical, coherent order. This should be fun as you actually see the appropriate organization emerge. Now, you will understand why we suggest this creative process and why it works. It encourages you to pick up innovative ideas from a variety of sources which in all likelihood never would have occurred to you if you had just gone about writing your speech in the routine way from beginning to end.

*

In case you are wondering when you actually begin writing the speech, be patient. You will begin that process just after you divide all your papers into three piles—introduction, body, and conclusions. After arranging them logically, you can start to write, adding the appropriate connecting phrases and paragraphs.

*

Avoid writing the introduction first. Again, trust our system. Write the body of your speech, then the conclusion, and finally the introduction. Imagine that your speech is a rich, juicy apple pie which you are creating from scratch. The filling, or in this case, the body of your speech, is the most important part. Decide what that should be, pack it with substance, and do it first. Following that, you more naturally will be able to form a compatible, strong base (the conclusion) and a mouth watering, attractive top crust (the introduction).

*

As you write the body of your presentation, always remember that a speech is not a term paper on its hind legs. It is a special form of communication which has its own rhythm and style. For example, contractions such as *isn't, he's* or *shouldn't* are frowned upon in written communication, but are commonplace, and often preferred, when talking. Put them in your speech.

*

Use short words and sentences, direct nouns and verbs; avoid drawn-out descriptions unless you are making a special point. It is not necessary to agree with Ronald Reagan's politics to envy his communication skills. An analysis of his speeches shows that more than ninety percent of the words contain only one or two syllables. Long words and involved sentences in a speech are difficult to understand; they also can be traps over which even the best speaker bumbles or stumbles.

*

Avoid jargon, technical, or business language. Disregard this rule only if you are sure your audience will understand, or more important, if you know they expect this type of mumbo-jumbo. When in doubt, use standard English. These words are not verbs: *inventory, interface, input,* or *brainstorm. Planning-wise, health-wise,* and *speech-wise* are no-no's; *clockwise, otherwise,* and *lengthwise* are fine.

*

Always keep a dictionary and a thesaurus at your side. They are invaluable sources of pronunciation as well as a help in expanding your vocabulary. Do not be as concerned with spelling unless you are giving away copies of your presentation.

*

Choose no more than three key points for the substance or body of your speech, and stick to them. If you are fortunate enough to have too much material, edit, and be somewhat ruthless about it. You want those three points to stand out.

*

Consult the library, a colleague, or other sources if some of your material is too skimpy or you obviously lack certain facts. Remember, we told you to be patient. Now you can see how much time and frustration you have saved by waiting to undertake research until you finally know what you do not know.

*

Gather all the rest of your information and fit it into your speech to close the gaps. You have now written a rough draft of the body of your presentation. It has three cogent ideas which have been expanded sufficiently but not to infinity. It is in a clear style to be spoken, not read. Now, you are ready for the next step—writing the conclusion. Remember, do not touch the introduction, even though you may be thinking about it. Leave that for last, and you will find to your delight that it nearly writes itself.

*

Write your finale with care. This is your last chance to impress your audience and you should leave them with a thought or two they will long remember.

*

Do not reveal you are an amateur by stopping your oral presentation abruptly. Just because you have said everything you want to say, do not end with, *I guess that's it, thank you and good day.* Even worse, do not drag in new or irrelevant material, adding lamely, *Oh, yes, I nearly forgot.*

*

Summarize the main points of your presentation (remember, only three), and then add a personal touch or appeal for action which will stir your listeners. *This is what I intend to do, and I urge you to join me—We need to get the word out to our friends and neighbors, and I volunteer—I truly believe this is the best course of action and that we are the company to do it.*

*

Include a memorable quote or favorite stanza of poetry only if it is appropriate to your subject and you feel comfortable about it. If you never read Shakespeare—or you know your audience doesn't—do not trot out the Bard just for this occasion.

*

Reject the temptation to conclude by thanking people for their attention. If you have been successful, they will thank you. If you haven't, don't remind them.

*

Now you have completed two of the three sections of your presentation. It is time to prepare the introduction. It should consist of thoughts you did not use when writing the body and conclusion as well as other ideas that have been percolating along in the back of your brain this last week or so.

*

Remember that the purpose of the introduction is to capture the attention of your audience. Your opening sentences convince them that you are worthy of being listened to and lead them expectantly into the main part of your speech.

*

Write your introduction so that it immediately captures the attention of this particular group of listeners. This is sure to get them to listen, *Ten years from now twenty percent of us in this room will have died or be seriously ill of lung cancer.* Or, begin with a question: *How many of you know that the United States has one of the highest infant mortality rates in the world?* You might start with a story: *When I was growing up, my mother always made a steaming bowl of oatmeal for my breakfast. Today, most children are lucky to have cold cereal.* Or use a familiar quotation. *Franklin Roosevelt said, 'We have nothing to fear but fear itself.'*

*

You may begin by thanking the person who introduced you and saying how happy you are to be there—but be brief. This is not the time to pay back all your debts.

*

Do not insult yourself or your audience by making excuses. Never, never write an introduction which says, *I don't know why you asked me—I'm not really a public speaker—I hope you will all bear with me.* We all have heard speakers who seem to think they must be super humble and apologize for everything—for just being there, for presuming to talk on the subject, for not being the Nobel laureate on the issue. If you have nothing worthwhile to say, your audience will find that out soon enough.

*

Never talk up or down to your audience. Use words you know they understand in the context they understand.

*

If you are substituting for someone else at the last minute, do not whine, *I wish I had had more time to prepare, but I'll do the best I can at this short notice.* This disparages the chairperson and loses the sympathy and gratefulness of the audience. Take charge as if you would like nothing more than to be there at this time and place. They will be so charmed and delighted that the next time, they will ask you first. End your introduction by leading into the body of your presentation. *I will cover three points today, one . . ., two . . ., and three.*

*

Follow much of these same organizational procedures for a shorter talk, though you may want to cover no more than two main points.

*

It may come somewhat as a surprise, but having followed these rules, you have written your whole speech. It is twenty to thirty minutes long and contains no more than three cogent points. The introduction causes the audience to sit up and take notice, the body gives them information they would never hear elsewhere or, if commonplace, is presented in a unique way. The conclusion rouses them to action. But that's only on paper. Remember, this is not a written exercise, it is a speech. You now need to start practicing so that your oral delivery is worthy of your written material.

* * *

3

Use It or Lose It

TECHNIQUES OF DELIVERY

The most common means of delivering a speech are either to read from a manuscript, memorize the entire text, or paraphrase notes on cards. As you become a more experienced speaker, we hope that you will be able to organize your material so you can reduce the contents of your speech to three notecards—one each for your introduction, body, and conclusion. However, most of us who give only an occasional speech do best by writing it all out and practicing until we can recite whole paragraphs or thoughts with ease. That is the technique we follow in this book, although we recommend the notecard approach, particularly for presentations of ten minutes or less. Whatever your method, the key to successful delivery is practice, practice, and more practice. Follow these steps to success.

*

Type your finished speech double spaced in capital letters. Never staple or bind the pages together. You want to turn the pages as unobtrusively as possible. But there is always the danger of dropping them. This points out the value of using a few note cards.

*

This is the third week of preparation—and just a week or so before you give your speech. You have spent the first week gathering your thoughts and the second week writing. In the best of all worlds, you have a week to perfect your oral delivery. If you have less time, you will have to work harder.

*

Begin practicing by reading your entire text into a tape recorder. You probably will have to slow down your normal conversational speed to about one hundred and seventy words per minute. If you do not have a timer, a good rule of thumb is to remember that one typed double spaced page has about two hundred and fifty words; in a good oral delivery, this should take about ninety seconds.

*

Replay the tape as many times as you need. Listen carefully. Does your speech have an oral quality? Consider: Are your sentences short and succinct? If not, cut them down. Is your message getting bogged down? Add transitional words such as *and, and so,* or *therefore.* Are you stumbling over big words? Choose a more simple alternative. Unless you are talking to a technical audience that is impressed only by three syllable words not found in an ordinary dictionary, speak in plain English. Use a simple test. If you were listening, would you be attentive? Would your subordinates? Your boss? A group that never met you before?

*

Practice!

If you can find an honest critic who knows something about public speaking, ask his or her assistance to listen and give advice. Unfortunately, most spouses, secretaries, or colleagues cannot be objective enough to be much help. Either they are too critical, or not critical enough. Most likely, you are on your own, so heed our advice carefully.

*

Make appropriate changes in the text that clarify your message and express just what you want to say. Underline the words or phrases you will emphasize. Never use a word that is unfamiliar to you or that you have the slightest trouble pronouncing. You will be sure to flub it when you are in front of an audience.

*

Do not linger over unimportant words such as *the, a,* or *and*—never pronounce *the* as *thē*. For smoother delivery, use conjunctions—*they're* instead of *they are; we've* in place of *we have.*

*

Vary your pace. Speed up—and slow down—as the text requires.

*

Make note of places where gestures and other physical acts are appropriate, and practice them in front of a mirror. If you can do it with ease, point your finger—wave your glasses—hold up an object. Use gestures that make your presentation more interesting and help emphasize key points—but make sure they are natural to you. If you never wave your hand, do not program yourself to do it now. It will look as unnatural as you feel.

*

Time your speech. It should be no more than thirty minutes, and you should have covered three major points. Be ruthless in eliminating extraneous words and phrases. If they still seem important, do not throw them in the wastebasket; gather them up to save for another speech or the question and answer period which follows.

*

Listen carefully to the pitch of your voice. Keep it well-modulated and in the low range. High voices lack a sense of authority and are irritating to listeners. Unless you are a trained singer, you cannot alter your natural pitch radically, but if you tend to squeak when you are excited or nervous, tone it down as much as possible. Follow the hints in Chapter 6, *Antidotes for Wobbly Knees and Sweaty Palms* to control uncontrollable symptoms.

*

Become especially familiar with the contents of your introduction and conclusion, and try to deliver them verbatim. This will enable you to concentrate on the audience at the most crucial times.

*

Rehearse your speech until you know it so well that you can look up at your audience more times than you look down at your script. But just as you probably wrote the speech in snatches, you probably do not have a large block of time to devote to perfecting its oral quality. Take a few minutes whenever you can, but do not let any day go by without going over it at least once. You do not want to lose your momentum.

*

Try to practice at least once in the room in which you will be speaking. If that is not possible, replicate that environment as much as possible. For example, you can simulate a podium with a pile of books, a microphone with a short statue or a lamp. If you are using visual aids, always rehearse with them beforehand.

*

By following our advice and dividing your speech-making chores into manageable segments—one week to gather thoughts, another to write, and the last week to practice your delivery—you have given yourself enough time to perfect your presentation. No need to panic; you are ready for your big day.

* * *

4

The Joke Never Is On You

HUMOR AND STORY TELLING

Most of us do not aspire to be a Will Rogers or a Joan Rivers. During the Great Depression, Rogers used story telling and homespun humor to get across a very definite point of view which charmed millions of people. In the eighties, Rivers also attracts a large audience, employing an outrageous, insulting style to comment upon the mores of her own day. Although most of us are not stand-up comics nor even armchair humorists, we do enjoy a good joke or an apt story, and audiences do, too.

But if you have never told a story well in your life, do not feel compulsively that now that you are giving a formal speech, you must insert it somewhere. It would be better for you—and the audience—to play it straight without the agony of a story poorly told. If, however, after some practice, you can be a raconteur, take advantage of that skill and use it appropriately.

*

Remember that the joke or story must be appropriate to the subject or theme of your speech. It can be placed anywhere—at the introduction to catch the attention of the audience, in the middle to enliven a somewhat ordinary presentation, or at the end to add just the right humorous or scintillating touch.

*

A twist on a familiar subject often works well and does not require you to learn a whole story. For example, if you are talking about what is wrong with education today you might begin, *I think every American child should learn a second language—English.*

*

Use anecdotes to express your humanity and common touch. The best ones are directed toward yourself and show that you, too, seemingly so self-assured, have had some failures. *The first time I was turned down for a job I learned a valuable lesson . . . My children are probably like yours. They like to argue, and I don't always have the right answer. But . . .* If you can build a common bond between you and the audience, they are more likely to listen to what you have to say.

*

Be nostalgic, but not maudlin. *Down on the farm, when I was a child, I learned my first lessons in making compromises,* is better than *The farm was a special place where I never minded doing chores because I knew my father worked much harder.* No one will believe the latter.

*

Never single out an ethnic, racial, or religious group. Such humor is not funny and always in bad taste.

*

Do not use dialect or a foreign accent. It classifies you as an insensitive bore.

*

Never begin by saying, *I heard a funny story the other day.* The audience may not agree it is funny at all and wonder about your perverse sense of humor. The remark, *This reminds me of . . .* is a more acceptable transition. Better still, just tell it without the introduction.

*

Resist the temptation to laugh at your own joke, though you may smile in a friendly, knowing manner.

*

Do not present a story or joke you do not know perfectly.

*

Write it all down, or at the least, the punchline. That is the part you are most likely to forget in time of panic.

*

Never give a speech consisting of a string of jokes or anecdotes connected with short phrases. Pepper your remarks appropriately if it suits you, but never at the expense of your subject. If the audience wanted to hear a comic, they would have asked for one.

* * *

5

Replace Your Thousand Words with a Picture

MASTERING VISUAL AIDS

Today's audiences are tuned into receiving considerable information from television, a medium where the visual impact is as important as the spoken word. A speaker who is skillful in the use of graphic material has another tool to keep the audience's attention, and increases the likelihood it will retain his message.

The most common visual aids are movies, slides and film strips, videotapes, graphs, and charts. Whatever technique you choose, make sure your materials are of the highest quality and that you are completely familiar with their context—and the equipment. Never expect your host to have everything together, and assume something will go wrong if it possibly can. Most important, be prepared to make your presentation without any visual aids at all if the power goes out or other misfortunes occur.

*

Select your visual material with these criteria in mind: the purpose of your speech, the type of audience, and its level of understanding of the subject.

*

Choose your visual material with you in mind. Never use any illustration with which you are not familiar.

*

Know your material so well that you can concentrate on the audience.

*

Do not use reproductions from books or reports unless they are equally effective in a larger medium. In fact, as a general rule, they are incomprehensible when enlarged and should not be used. Have an artist develop special illustrations, or do them yourself. Even a freehand drawing is more acceptable than a chart with microscopic numbers and words.

*

Never use inferior material for which you need to apologize. If it is unsatisfactory, do not show it.

*

Come early so you can check out the room. Bring your own equipment whenever possible, and make sure it is in working order. If you have to rely on a machine strange to you, always go through a dry run beforehand. Locate the electrical outlets, light switches, and microphones, and make sure they work. Take along extension cords; extra pads of paper; light bulbs for slide or movie projectors; tape, tacks, pointers, chalk, and crayon and felt tip pens for blackboards or charts.

*

Always place the screen or chart in the front and center of the room. Use a pointer, or a pen or pencil, and stand off to the side and face the audience. This may take some practice, as your natural impulse will be to address the materials in back of you by facing them, and thus turning your back on the audience. This not only blocks their view of the screen, but breaks the personal relationship you must maintain.

*

Check out all your graphics before the meeting begins. Do not use anything that cannot be seen or is not readable from the last row in the audience.

*

If at all possible, have an assistant to run the equipment so that you can concentrate on your presentation.

*

Do everything you can to forestall catastrophe. Lock your slides in place in the tray; have your film threaded or your videotape ready to go. Number slides or transparencies on the back so they can be reshuffled easily if they get scrambled.

*

If you are using a chalkboard, or an easel and paper, write legibly in large letters.

*

Except for a very small group, use a microphone, especially in a darkened room. Audiences are lulled to sleep easily by a droning, soft voice they barely hear.

*

Use handouts when you have more to say than you can handle orally. They are like security blankets. They relieve the audience of the obligation of remembering everything on the spot, and give you the opportunity to give them a message they can carry home. But avoid giving out a lengthy treatise that most likely will be thrown away. One or two pages should be sufficient.

*

If your handout is a mere summary of your remarks, and you are not going to refer to it in your presentation, do not distribute it until you are through speaking. Nothing distracts an audience more quickly than the temptation to rattle pages to try to keep up with the speaker.

*

If you refer to the handout in your talk, make sure your audience has it beforehand—either by giving it out at the door or by leaving a paper on each empty seat before the meeting begins.

*

If you have several handouts, try the kindergarten approach which works even with sophisticated audiences— color code them. You will avoid much pain, and anguish, and help people find their place by saying *Let's turn to page three—that's the orange sheet.*

*

Always assume one-third or one-half of the audience will lose or misplace the material. Have extra copies on hand.

*

Never allow any prop to overpower your speech. It is better to have nothing at all than to use it poorly. Visual aids can enhance your presentation and complement what you say. They can add zip and interest to your oral presentation, but only if you coordinate them with your remarks, and remain in control. They are not a shortcut to good public speaking. If in doubt, don't. You still have your vocal gifts to carry you through.

* * *

6

Antidotes for Wobbly Knees and Sweaty Palms

No matter how prepared you are, public speaking always has a degree of spontaneity and unpredictability. That is because it is a live situation involving real people, whose feelings and reactions never can be anticipated absolutely. It is the exact opposite of a movie or a videotape where the director and the editor can eliminate the glitches by doing re-takes, or cutting and splicing. When you give an oral presentation, any mistake you make is right there for all to see and hear. On the other hand, if you do a good job, you reap instant recognition and approval.

Even so, no matter how well we may be prepared, when the day, hour, and minute finally arrives, we are likely to:

* Gasp for air, sure that our lungs and salivary glands have long since stopped functioning.

* Wonder how to handle nausea or a fainting spell when the large intestine succeeds in its efforts to strangle the small one.

* Feel sure that the deafening thump, thump, thump of our heart can be heard in the last row of the audience.

* Be afflicted with hands so sticky that, like Lady Macbeth's, they cannot be wiped dry.

* Feel like a disembodied spirit with no control over life or limb.

* Know for certain that our voice will be a few octaves higher, if we have any voice at all.

* Struggle to maintain good posture when our legs seem to have forgotten that their primary function is to support their body.

* See only an indefinable blur even though we can hear an audience breathing somewhere out there.

These symptoms are real, and they afflict even the most experienced speakers, but they need not be debilitating. Borrow a note from the winning football coach: the best defense is a good offense—or from the scouts: be prepared. Know your speech so well that you have the confidence to be able to react quickly and assuredly to anything that may happen.

If you have followed our advice so far, you have written a well organized, cogent, and interesting twenty to thirty minute speech. You have rehearsed it so that you own it.

You are as ready as you ever will be.

The time has come, and still, you are nervous. Remember, it is natural to have butterflies in your stomach. You just need to learn how to get them all to fly in the same direction. That's what this chapter is all about.

*

Check out the room beforehand. At the very least, come early. It is a truism that anything that can go wrong will go wrong, so you must strive to control your environment as much as possible.

*

Try to arrange the seating to your liking. At the least, put the shortest distance possible between you and the audience. Lower or raise the thermostat, adjust the podium and the microphone. Turn off the canned music. Locate the electrical outlets, if you are using visual aids, and the exits, in case of fire or panic. Ask someone to give you a pitcher of cold water and a glass.

*

If you are speaking after a meal, eat lightly but well. Protein such as eggs, cheese, fish, poultry, or meat will give you the most long-term energy. Avoid heavy sauces and desserts that make you feel heavy and sleepy. Do not drink coffee, tea, or alcoholic beverages. They dry up the salivary glands and cloud the mind.

*

Remember that you are a speaker, not a musician. Control your fingers. Do not jingle coins or keys, or drum a martial beat on the stand.

*

If there is no speaker's podium, or you have trained yourself to speak without one, hold your speech in one hand and let the other hang loosely at your side or remain casually in your pocket.

*

You should have sent the chairperson a current biographical sketch, but even so, bring along another one in case he or she has forgotten. Better yet, write your own introduction. In many cases it will be the one that is used, and it says just what you want to be said about you.

*

After you are acknowledged, stand up, arrange yourself comfortably at the podium, and look around slowly at the audience. It may take awhile before all those faces come into focus, but take your time. You are in charge and they have nowhere to go.

*

Do not take your watch off and lay it ostentatiously on the podium. That is a signal to the audience that you are so poorly organized that you need an artifice to tell you when you are through.

*

If a few in the audience appear bored or distracted, never mind them. Do not waste your time trying to win them over by looking at them particularly or gesturing in their direction. Assume that their disaffection is caused by indigestion or a fight with the boss or spouse—in other words, nothing you can control. Concentrate your attention on the rest of those friendly and attentive faces.

*

Never, never start your speech by tapping the microphone and asking, *Is this on? Can you all hear me?* This immediately brands you as an amateur who should not, and will not, be taken seriously. You should have tested the microphone beforehand to make sure it is working. If a gremlin has pulled out the plug, you will know soon enough.

*

Always use a microphone, except in a very small room. It can help you project an intimate, conversational tone to everyone in the audience. Make sure you know everything there is to know about it. Practice lowering or raising it beforehand, assuming you may have to adjust it after the first person speaks.

*

Be prepared to act when the sound system acts up. It is known to wheeze and squeal at the most unfortuitous times. Refer the problem immediately to the person in charge or to the maintenance person. If there is one, you should have made his or her acquaintance before your speech. If any time will elapse before the sound system is repaired, go on without it. But speak up clearly.

*

Remember that a good sound system is very sensitive, and can be dangerous. Never say anything, even a whisper, within its range which may be confidential.

*

Stand tall, natural and relaxed, alert and vigorous. Do not slump, move tentatively from one foot to another, nor drape yourself over the lectern. Do balance yourself on both feet slightly apart and rest your hands on the podium—or one hand on the podium and another in your pocket. Hold onto your speech in front of you in a secure but not deathly grip.

*

Keep in mind that you have just two minutes to capture the audience's attention before it drifts away. Your text should recognize that, and so should your delivery. Give yourself the most assistance by memorizing the first three or four sentences of your speech so that you can concentrate on your surroundings and the listeners.

*

Smile. Your face should indicate a combination of warmth, friendliness, and authority. Convey the impression that you are an approachable, likeable human being with something important to say.

*

Do not drape yourself over the lectern

Let your voice rise and fall in accordance with your message. Vary the volume. If you shout everything, your audience will not be able to tell what is important; likewise, if you drone on and on in middle range, they will be bored. Whispers can be very effective in getting the audience to strain to hang onto your words—but do not whisper more than once or twice in your presentation.

*

Avoid any mannerisms which distract the audience from paying attention to your message. Do not take your eyeglasses off and put them on again unless you have planned this beforehand. Using glasses as a pointer, for example, can be an effective gesture.

*

Always maintain eye contact with your audience, moving your head naturally from side to side. But you can do this only if you know your speech so well that you will not lose your place when you glance up.

*

If you do lose your place, relax and breathe deeply. Take all the time necessary to regroup. It may seem like an hour, but most likely it will be just a few seconds until you find your place again. Do not worry about any negative reaction from the audience. They like you so well by now they will forgive—and may even think you planned—a pregnant pause. Avoid filling in the silence with junk words such as *ah, er, y'know,* or *okay.*

*

If your mind really does go blank and you cannot remember what to say next, follow these key rules: 1) keep talking even if you repeat what you just said; the audience will think you are merely emphasizing an important point and never realize you have forgotten what comes next. 2) Keep moving. Step forward, backward, or to the side. One or two steps in any direction will unfreeze you and get you going again. Never turn your back to the audience. 3) Jump ahead to another part of your presentation that you do remember. No one in the audience except a speech teacher will notice your somewhat jumbled organization. You should be sufficiently rehearsed and informed about your subject so you always have something to say. When you are off and running again, you can pick up the points you may have skipped.

*

Finally, no matter what has befallen you, the time speeds on and you near the end. Remember that second in difficulty to beginning the speech is finishing it. If you have taken our advice so far, you have written a good, snappy, attention-getting conclusion. Avoid the temptation to string it out because things are going so well you have begun to enjoy the limelight. Say what you have decided to say, and sit down gracefully.

*

Savor the applause and attention. You deserve it.

* * *

7

How to Answer Questions Without Catching Foot-In-Mouth Disease

Very few speeches are complete without a question and answer period. Consider it an integral part of your presentation—not an ordeal you hope to survive.

People ask questions because they: a) were not listening; b) want their own chance to pontificate; c) are eager to show up the speaker's inadequacies; or d) sincerely want more information.

Unless you know otherwise, always assume that each questioner has honorable motives; treat each one with respect.

You as the speaker are still in control, even though the question period should be somewhat informal. You already have gained credibility by your prepared remarks, and the audience is ready to believe nearly anything else you say.

Welcome the question and answer time as an opportunity to add ideas or information you were not able to include in your prepared remarks.

The person who has introduced you also should introduce the question and answer period, but if he or she is flustered, or does not know what to do, take the initiative. Always be prepared when you are expected to be unprepared. In other words, have a good idea what you would like to say. As you rehearse your written remarks, second guess the audience—jot down a half dozen or so most likely questions. What would you ask if you were they? With just a little effort, you can be remarkably clairvoyant because most people are predictable. Their questions will not be exactly like yours, but they should be close enough. Memorize short answers to the most likely questions. After your prepared remarks are over, you or your host may call a short recess after which you are prepared to answer questions.

*

State the ground rules. Set a time limit, no longer than your speech itself, for the entire question period; allow no one to ask a second question until everyone has had at least one turn (unless the second question is clearly a follow-up); accept questions, not statements from members of the audience; ask individuals to identify themselves.

*

If the subject is somewhat embarrassing—sexual information for teenagers—or controversial—how to get rid of the scoundrel in city hall—it may be prudent to allow anonymous written questions. If so, have someone help you sort them out. In general, however, oral questions move the meeting along and are more spontaneous.

*

Listen carefully to the questioner to detect any intent beyond the words. You are more likely to be able to do this if you have taken time beforehand to know the audience. For example, a query, "Who is going to pay for what you propose?" may require a different answer if it is asked by the president of the local bank than by the leader of a grassroots citizens organization.

*

Always repeat the question, or paraphrase it if it is long. This enables everyone to hear it, and gives you time to think up an answer. If you summarize a particularly lengthy question, politely check back and ask the individual, *Have I said it right?*

*

If many people are raising their hands and seeking recognition at the same time, ease their tension by recognizing the two or three you will call on next. *Let's see. We'll take Jane's question first; then the gentleman in the blue suit.*

*

Talk to the whole audience, not only the questioner. Look around the room to include them all, just as you did during your formal remarks.

*

Likewise, do not be so specific that your answer does not interest anyone else. If the question requires a direct or technical reply, keep the questioner satisfied and the audience happy by saying, *I'll be glad to answer you more thoroughly after the meeting. Please see me later.* Then be sure to meet the person afterward. He or she may forget, but you must not.

*

Remember, that no question deserves an encyclopedic response, at least at this time. A polite but terse *yes* or *no* may not only be the most appropriate response, but may defuse a tense situation.

*

If necessary, restate a point you covered in your main speech, but never by saying, *As I said before.* That makes the questioner feel stupid as if you are saying, *You should have understood the first time, but I'll repeat it for you.*

*

Do not fear a challenge from the floor. If you are correct, stand firm. If you are wrong, admit it. Always be polite. Never argue, lose your temper, nor insult the questioner so that he or she gains the natural sympathy of the audience that until now has been with you.

*

Do not fear a challenge from the floor

Use humor to deflect run-on or quarrelsome questioners. Audiences will respond favorably to your smiling answer, *You certainly have an interesting point of view. But since we don't have time for a full discussion, you'll have to be like my mother—trust me.*

*

If you really do not want to answer the question, take a cue from good politicians. Answer the question the way you want to, not necessarily how the questioner expected. If you are adroit you can bypass the crux of the matter completely. If anyone notices, he or she will be too polite to say something.

*

Do not be afraid to say honestly that you do not know the answer. Offer to look it up and get in touch with the questioner later.

*

Avoid the temptation to refer a difficult question to someone else in the audience. Never say, *Here's Ms. Bixby sitting in the corner. I'll bet she can answer this better than I can.* You will probably lose your bet and you may lose a friend. Chances are that Ms. Bixby: a) does not know; b) may know but does not want to share what she knows; and/or c) will never forgive you for singling her out.

*

If there is honest disagreement, say so. *Look, I know we don't agree. Many honest people do not. At this point, let's just agree to disagree.*

*

Stick to your time schedule and bow out as gracefully as you began. Briefly summarize your main points and say, *I see our time is up and I know most of you are eager to go home (or have lunch, or dinner, or just get out of there). Thank you very much.*

* * *

8

Short Remarks
that Say Something

So far in this book, we have given you pointers about how to give a polished oral presentation when you are the focus of attention, that is, the featured speaker.

But as a manager, executive, or program chairperson, you most likely will be given the task—at a meeting, conference, or social event—either of introducing someone else who has center stage or of making only a few well chosen remarks.

Do not spurn this second banana role. It gives you the opportunity to practice another set of skills. It is a considerable art to have the right words in just the right amount of time, if only for a short while. Prepare and rehearse carefully. On each of these occasions, make the most out of the opportunity—for yourself.

WELCOME. As the representative of the group, you have the privilege to extend greetings to an honored guest. Begin with words about the appropriateness or significance of the occasion. *It is our custom each spring to give this special award to a special person.* Then compliment the individual recipient with a personal and/or biographical remark. *We are so pleased that you are following in the footsteps of your father and grandfather who also had great love for this institution and whom we honored in years past.* Keep your tone warm and friendly, as if you were greeting the person in your own home. You are, indeed, the host or hostess for the occasion.

FAREWELL. You may be representing a group in saying goodbye to someone else or speaking for yourself. If you or the speaker are leaving willingly, the occasion may be somewhat sad and nostalgic. If you or the person are not leaving under amicable circumstances, even though a formal farewell is expected, the situation can be embarrassing. No matter. You and the audience are carrying out a ritual. The occasion calls for tact and politeness and no mention of past animosities which may have caused the parting. Talk only of superficial pleasantries, and if it is appropriate, of tasks accomplished and deeds well done. Wish the honoree well in his or her new undertaking, even if you are delighted the individual is leaving. If you yourself are leaving under somewhat clouded circumstances, be gracious. You soon will be gone.

PRESENTATION. Someone is being rewarded or honored on a happy occasion for all concerned. In this case, fulsome praise and exaggeration are warranted and even expected. If you are presenting a scroll or a plaque, do not bore the audience by reading an awkward text word-for-word; paraphrase it instead. Say something about the history of the award and the criteria for winning. Add additional laudatory information about the honoree, and his or her accomplishments. Before you introduce the judges, find out if the rules call for anonymity. If a gift is being presented, do not give the honoree the impossible task of struggling with an awkwardly wrapped package. Make sure it can be easily undone. If, by chance, the award has not arrived when the time comes, have something—at the very least, a nicely printed piece of paper—to present to the honoree. Never have nothing. Lead the hearty applause.

ACCEPTANCE. In this instance, you are the recipient of an award or honor. If you are supposed to be surprised, act surprised, even though a well meaning friend leaked the news to you a week before to make sure you would be present. Unfortunately, the demeanor of many Academy Award winners are examples of what not to do. Resist the temptation to share the honor by modestly thanking everyone you can think of who helped you get where you are today. The audience does not care and probably will not recognize their names. Do thank groups in general—*my family, my staff,* and then, *one or two very special people* . . . *my third grade teacher, Miss Able, who taught me the value of persistence,* or *my mother, who believed in me when others did not.* Be sincerely appreciative, and if possible, tell the audience what you are going to do with the reward. *This will enable me to continue my studies in molecular biology. Thank you all very much.* If you have any idea you are going to be given an award, prepare and memorize brief remarks beforehand. Be gracious to the losers.

INTRODUCING THE MAIN EVENT. Remember that the purpose of your remarks is to promote the credibility of the speaker, not your own. You are not the main attraction. Even so, this does not relieve you of the responsibility of being organized and interesting. If the speaker bombs, yours may be the only words the audience remembers.

Tailor your tone to the mood of the occasion. If the speaker is a well known comedian here to entertain the group, be light and frivolous in your remarks. If he or she is talking about the dangers of nuclear war, be equally as serious in your introduction.

*

Be succinct. You know you do not believe the trite, *Our speaker needs no introduction,* so do not say it. You have a role to play, but it is not to drone on and on incessantly, beginning with the speaker's birth and recounting every event since then.

*

Ask for a written biographical resume in advance, and then prepare your remarks by embellishing the hard facts with personal information. You can pique the audience's interest if you say, *He attended high school right here in our town before he won the Nobel prize, and says if it wasn't for his math teacher he wouldn't be where he is today.*

*

Divide your introduction into the same three parts as you would any speech—introduction, body and conclusion. First, include remarks that capture the attention of the audience, *If a nuclear bomb were dropped on our community, all civilization as we know it would perish.* Say something about the subject and why it is appropriate to talk about it at this time. Then, discuss the speaker— who he is, where he comes from, why he is the right person to make the address. Indicate any honors he has been given which establish his legitimacy to be with you at this time. Indicate his human qualities—hobbies or special interests. Conclude by a simple statement, *We are honored to have a nationally known expert in this field,* _____.

*

Choose information which enhances the speaker's credibility to talk on this subject at this time and ignore the inappropriate. He may have been an Eagle Scout, but unless this increases his stature with this particular audience, forget it. The specific reference, *Her work on the economics of a small business is particularly relevant to those of us in the same boat* is better than the generality, *She has had many experiences with small business—but I'll let her tell you about them.*

*

Neither damn the speaker with faint praise—*He is so well known, nothing more I can say will do him justice* —nor embarrass him with too much. If he or she is famous or notorious, do not gush or be overawed like a smitten teenager.

*

Compose your introduction beforehand, and practice it, much as you would an entire speech if you were the headliner.

*

Be sure you pronounce the speaker's name correctly. If it is a tongue twister, write it out phonetically.

*

Do not talk about yourself. *I remember when Bill was in town last and we were talking about this same subject. It is my opnion that* .... This not only bores your audience but may get them to murmuring, "Who does he think he is? We didn't come here to hear what he thinks."

*

Lead the applause as the speaker rises; lead the applause when he or she finishes.

*

Decide beforehand whether you or the speaker will take questions from the audience; avoid the awkward "you first, no, you first" routine.

*

At the question and answer period, detour an embarrassing silence by being prepared to ask the first question.

*

End on time with a pithy summary and a sincere thank you.

*

SETTING THE SCENE. If you are introducing the after-dinner speaker following a formal banquet, you most likely will introduce the head table as well. More gaffes are made in this type of oral communication than any other. Resist the temptation to be cute or wordy. It is better to say too little than too much. Follow this procedure to handle such situations with grace.

*

Facing the audience, seat the speaker immediately to the left of the podium. You should sit to the right of the speaker's stand. When the time comes for introductions, a good rule to follow is to go from the outside in. Start at your far right and go down the line, saying a few appropriate words about each person at the head table. Then begin at your far left and do the same. Avoid the awkwardness of ignoring the speaker completely, but do not introduce him or her at length at this point; indicate you will have more to say in a few minutes.

*

Remember that nothing is more sacred to a person than his or her name. Be sure you pronounce each one correctly. There are traps everywhere so check with each one, unless you know them well. Even John Smith may pronounce his name Smythe.

*

Identify each individual by title, rank, or some personal but inoffensive description, giving each one equal billing. Single out only the speaker for a detailed introduction—afterwards.

*

Be consistent in your address. Mary Jones may be married, but she is not an appendage to her husband, and thus, not likely to care to be Mrs. John Jones. To save time, if they are sitting next to each other, you may introduce them both together as John and Mary Jones. But then, still say something personal: *As you may know, John is our company's president and Mary is a well known sculptor.*

*

Bite your tongue if you are tempted to say, *Last but not least.* The last may or may not be the least. Avoid it.

*

Be firm about insisting that members of the audience hold their applause until the whole group is introduced.

*

Save the head table the embarrassment of having to fumble with napkins, water glasses, and the like in order to rise after being introduced. Ask them to remain seated and nod their acknowledgement.

*

Take no more than five minutes for the whole affair.

*

Lead the applause for everyone when you are through.

*

TOASTING, NOT ROASTING. There are many occasions —weddings, special anniversaries, birthdays, retirement parties—when a toast is in order. If you have any reason to believe you will be called upon, prepare for it and follow the general formula we suggest in the section on introductions. But since the occasion calls for wit and spontaneity, memorize what you want to say. This is one time in public speaking when hyperbole, extreme rhetoric, and exaggeration are acceptable and even appropriate. Still, make your words brief and meaningful.

If you are asked to give a toast at the last moment and cannot think of anything specific to say about the honoree, tailor an anecdote or story that you may know to fit this occasion. The audience is likely to be in a jovial mood, and will laugh or appreciate anything you say.

In summary, on those occasions where a short presentation is called for, have confidence that you can rise to the occasion. Succinct, well articulated remarks will bring you distinction.

* * *

9

When You're Moved
to Respond

FORMULA FOR IMPROMPTU SPEAKING

How often have we watched in awe as an individual gets up to speak after being asked to say a few words and delivers an oration in the same league as the Gettysburg Address?

You, too, may be invited to a social or political gathering where you can shine as an extemporaneous speaker. The host or hostess may have given out little clues that you will be welcome to say a few words, or may even be amenable to a subtle suggestion from you or a friend. On other occasions, you may find yourself in a situation where there is an opportunity to volunteer some well-turned phrases.

Whenever you have any warning, by all means formulate your thoughts beforehand. On those few occasions when you truly have no notice, be calm. The audience knows you have just been called upon and will not expect a polished orator. Have confidence also that you can rely upon your previous experience and knowledge of the subject, as well as the speech making skills you have learned in this book, to make a credible presentation.

Always be prepared to appear to be unprepared.

*

Do not apologize or appear to put down the chairperson by saying, *I never expected to be called on, or I would have thought out what I wanted to say.* Everyone knows that.

*

Always be prepared to be "unprepared"

Even if you are expected to respond immediately to the chairperson's remarks, "I see Hank in the audience, and I know we'd like to hear his ideas on the subject," take your time. Move to the front of the room slowly, clear your throat, put your hand in your pocket, look around— all the while assembling your thoughts.

*

Keep at the ready some key phrases, punchy remarks or a story or two which can come trippingly off your tongue and be altered on the spot to fit the occasion.

*

Put your remarks in a context familiar to your audience by referring to social, economic, or political matters understood by them.

*

Discuss only those aspects of the issue with which you are particularly familiar.

*

Whenever possible, refer to the remarks of previous speakers, either on the platform or in the audience, and then add your own points. This not only gives credibility to what you say and shows you were listening, but also may give you the opportunity to bring about consensus and agreement on an important matter.

*

Take this opportunity to point out the advantages and disadvantages of solutions to certain problems and then propose your own.

*

Avoid sarcasm and derogatory remarks, no matter how much right you have on your side.

*

Keep to the subject and never speak off the cuff more than three minutes. The audience will be surprised if you can be eloquent that long, but suspicious and hostile that you may have a hidden agenda if you ramble on and on.

* * *

10

There Is a Difference

WOMEN SPEAKERS

While the principles discussed in the rest of this book can be followed with equal success by men and women, we would be remiss if we did not devote some time to discussing the unique attributes that women offer in the field of oral communication. Perhaps in the best of all possible worlds there would be no differences between men and women speech makers. But there are—and we need to understand and make the most of the positive attributes.

Up to the age of twenty-one, females are superior to males in the use of language. Until recently, their skills reached a plateau when most women married and spent the next twenty years of their lives looking after a household and rearing children. Thus, while most men went out into the world and were forced to increase their language skills in order to survive, the women stayed home and were not subject to the same communication challenges. Homemaking is a fine profession, and children have many qualities, but looking after their needs does not require the specialized oral communication techniques of the professional and business world.

Today, however, the western woman has become a force to consider in corporate and business life. She is competitive with the man, with all the assets and liabilities connected with that new role.

In terms of oral communication—the ability to make others understand what you are saying and to believe in you as the appropriate messenger of the information— the female has several advantages over the male. She has:

* better command and love of language—poetry, literature, and the spoken and written word.
* fortunate tendency to personalize experiences. As Aristotle noted centuries ago, personal truth, or truth which comes from human experience, is a great asset in helping people reach a common ground of understanding and agreement.
* disciplined and systematic approach to organization; studies show that women select and arrange materials more effectively than men.
* patience, perseverance, and willingness to spend the time necessary to practice and perfect a program or presentation.

The truth notwithstanding, women have long been perceived as inferior, or at least not equal, to men. An effective woman speaker considers this a singular asset. She turns to her advantage the tendency of most audiences to favor the underdog.

To enhance her inherent positive qualities, and excel in oral communication, the female speaker should put her greatest emphasis in these areas: 1) using her voice; 2) reacting well to the question and answer period; 3) overcoming a natural unwillingness to confront issues that require confrontation; and 4) being especially conscious of dress and appearance.

USE OF THE VOICE. Female voices tend to be more highly pitched and less pleasant sounding to ears accustomed to the lower registers of the male. Yet, they also are more conversational and less formal. If you have serious vocal problems, you can engage a voice coach or take a diction course at your local university or community college. You also may learn yoga and other meditation exercises that help lessen stress. Chances are you do not need these formal and time consuming activities, because your voice most likely is pleasant enough, if you will learn to relax and use it to its full advantage. A practical technique that works is to read your speech into a tape recorder—a step-by-step routine we recommend for all speakers in Chapter 3, *Use It or Lose It—Techniques of Delivery.* The woman who may be less accustomed to public speaking will find this especially helpful. You soon will detect the nuances that make your way of talking special, and can train yourself to improve and highlight your best qualities.

The general conversational quality of a woman's voice is an asset. It engages rather than alienates the listener. Because of this, you probably would be less successful in formal debate, but chances are, you are not competing in that arena. Talk with people rather than to them by using words such as *we* and *our* rather than *you* and *your.* A friendly and engaging tone can help bridge the oftentimes cold gap between the listeners and the speaker.

THE QUESTION AND ANSWER PERIOD. Though Chapter 7, *How to Answer Questions Without Catching Foot-In-Mouth Disease,* deals with this subject at some length, there are special areas of particular interest to the woman speaker. As we have said, the wise speaker, male or female, prepares for the question period by anticipating a half dozen or so likely questions and formulating appropriate answers.

All speakers should consider this time after their formal remarks as an opportunity to focus on the audience's agenda while always keeping the meeting under control. But because most audiences still are more ready to accept the authority of a male speaker over a female, the woman speaker is likely to have to overcome this disadvantage. Even though the members of the audience may have been won over by an especially fine speech by a woman, they may still rationalize to themselves that that is because she had all the time in the world to prepare. They may remain somewhat skeptical that she can hold her own—or better yet, excel, in the free-for-all question period. In addition to our general techniques, the following are especially important to helping the woman speaker maintain and enhance her credibility.

*

Answer the first two or three questions at some length. This establishes your command over the issues and makes it clear that you are authoritative, credible and mature, and know far more than your prepared remarks may have indicated.

*

Accord each questioner respect. This is more natural for women than for men, and the audience will know it, and react favorably.

*

Take advantage of the more informal conversational mode in the question period. A woman's tendency to naturalness, liveliness, and humanity are real assets.

*

POSITIVE USE OF CONFRONTATION. Studies indicate that in general, women tend to act passively in the presence of men. While men feel free to interrupt women, women do not feel free to interrupt men. This is changing as women become leaders and executives in their own right. Still, women are more likely than men to try to move a conversation or situation toward consensus and away from confrontation. This is a valuable trait and may in time be a positive force in changing our values and attitudes toward solving problems. Still, there are times when confrontation, or at the least heated differences, can be positive, if they are used properly.

*

If you are faced with an especially antagonistic or hostile questioner, listen carefully, and make sure he or she knows you are listening. Lean forward, or look at the person intently; make it clear you are interested but not intimidated.

*

Respond in a firm, quiet tone; this is far easier for a woman than a man. Do not allow yourself to be interrupted. Say politely, but firmly: *I gave you the floor, sir. Now it is my turn.* The audience will be on your side if the questioner tries to take issue with you.

*

Summarize what has been said, and then advance the matter constructively. *As I understand what you said, you believe we're all off track and should fire everyone who is responsible. It seems to me that another factor to consider is how long it takes us to be profitable again with a whole group of new people.* Note how carefully you have summarized the individual's bombastic argument, and thus given him or her some credence, and yet given the discussion a far more positive turn.

*

Show by your demeanor that you are an individual people can trust. You listen carefully, sum up ideas skillfully, and guide the conversation or discussion to higher levels.

*

APPEARANCE. Though all speakers should be neat and presentable, this is an especially important consideration for a woman. Since you probably are somewhat new to your leadership role, and your audience, too, is unaccustomed to women in positions of authority, you must establish your credibility even before you speak.

*

If in doubt, wear more formal rather than less formal attire. A suit and neat blouse are always acceptable. The skirt should fit well when you sit down. This is an often overlooked factor you should practice at home in front of a mirror—or better yet, in the store dressing room before you buy.

*

Choose only the most complimentary colors, but nothing outrageous or outstanding. After their initial favorable impression, you want members of the audience to concentrate more on the contents—your presentation—than the package—what you look like.

*

Choose simple jewelry. Never wear bracelets that dangle, rings that glisten, or earrings which sway in the light breeze of indoor air conditioning.

*

Wear comfortable but attractive shoes. It is impossible to be alert and prepared if your toes pinch or your feet ache.

*

It does make a difference

If possible, wear a skirt or jacket with pockets. Men can stand casually and comfortably with one hand in their pocket because their clothes always have pockets. It is a very good position for a woman, too.

In summary, as a woman executive or professional person, you have a number of assets—especially in regard to language skills, perseverance and discipline—that can help you be an outstanding speaker. The more you use them effectively, the more self confident and effective you will be. The essential nature of the communicative act—even the most formal presentation—is to establish a trusting relationship between human beings. With training and practice, women can advance and enhance that relationship very well.

* * *

11

Ten Commandments
of Public Speaking

1. You cannot not communicate—*so do it well.*

2. Remember—*people are persuaded by people, not by information.*

3. Organize or orbit—*get it all together.*

4. Do not reinvent life—*use common phrases and experiences.*

5. Do what comes naturally to you—*tell a joke or a story only when it fits.*

6. Own the speech or it owns you—*practice makes permanent.*

7. Analyze the audience—*not yourself.*

8. Control your territory—*use every facility to advantage.*

9. Pull out the props—*always be prepared when your mind goes blank.*

10. Ecstacy comes after agony—*everyone has butterflies: successful speakers teach them to fly in one direction.*

12

What Have You Forgotten?

LAST MINUTE CHECKLIST

Does your speech meet your specific objectives?

- ☐ Provides information
- ☐ Elicits approval or support
- ☐ Helps promote understanding of a difficult or complex subject
- ☐ Projects favorable image of yourself or your company or organization

Does your speech meet the needs of the audience?

- ☐ Avoids jargon and difficult vocabulary
- ☐ Informs, persuades, or entertains
- ☐ Promotes understanding and respect for subject and for speaker

Is your speech twenty to thirty minutes long and does it contain:

- ☐ Introduction which arouses interest
- ☐ Body which presents no more than three main points
- ☐ Memorable conclusion

Have you rehearsed until you are thoroughly familiar with the contents of your speech?

Have you noted gestures and other means which are natural to you and will keep the attention of the audience?

Do your visual aids support your speech, not overpower nor detract from it?

Are your visual aids appropriate for the sophistication of the audience and the skill of the speaker?

Do you know how to operate all your equipment? If possible, do you have an assistant?

Have typical or expected audience questions been anticipated and rehearsed?

Is the room ready and has it been checked out beforehand?

☐ Heat or air conditioner working properly
☐ Piped-in music turned off
☐ Electrical outlets located
☐ Light switch/dimmer located and working
☐ Seats arranged properly
☐ Microphone correct volume and height
☐ Water glass and pitcher

Are the seating, podium, and microphone where you want them?

Is all your equipment in working order and available?

- ☐ Extra extension cords and light bulbs for projectors
- ☐ Tape, tacks, pointers, felt tip pens, chalk
- ☐ Flip-charts; extra paper

An hour or less before your speech, have you eaten lightly, drunk no caffeine nor alcoholic beverages?

Have you made arrangements for adequate parking beforehand so you do not have to spend valuable time driving around looking for a parking place just before the speech?

Will you be there early enough to attend to any last minute details?

Do you have a biographical summary or other material about yourself which the introducer can use?

Do you have several copies of your speech?

Are you ready with a summary or press release in case the media is present?

Are handouts available to be distributed? Are there more than enough copies of everything?

Have you agreed with the chairperson about how questions will be handled?

If all the above is checked off, YOU ARE READY. GOOD LUCK!

* * *

3 1543 50010 5822

808.51
C676y

808.51
C676y

Cogan
You can talk
to (almost) any-
one about (almo-
st) anything

DATE D

DATE	
NO 8 '85	Allanne Melnychuk
AG 08 86	B. Moyer. Ac. Apt. Cen
FE 13 '87	Carolineron

Cressman Library
Cedar Crest College
Allentown, PA 18104